Title - In the Beginning from Prophecies of War
ISBN 13 - 978-1-955144-04-9
Composer - Andrew T Hanna
Graphic Design, Layout, & Artwork - Andrew T Hanna
Copyright - 2022
Genre - Progressive Rock, Jazz-Fusion, Jazz-Rock

In the Beginning

from Prophecies of War

Composed By – Andrew Hanna

Artwork & Layout – Andrew Hanna

ISBN (13) – 9781955144049

Genre – Jazz-Rock, Jazz Fusion, Prog-Rock

When
I began my senior
year at University of the
Arts, I was musically experimenting
with different ideas and concepts from genres
outside of the Jazz idiom. At that point in my
musical development, Bebop's limitations were fully realized.
From the limited number of meters, repetitive song forms, narrow
harmonic range, lack of solo development, lack of individuality, narrow
rhythmic range, and so forth.

All of my musical experimentation culminated in my senior thesis entitled Prophecies of War.
It not only served as an expression of my musical experimentation, but as a reaction to Academic Jazz. While at
the University of the Arts, I noticed this bizarre notion of what constituted Jazz. Oddly, it was touted that
Jazz was the music created between the years 1945-1960. This narrow scope of Jazz conflicted with my his-
torical understanding of Jazz, which that genre began sometime in the early 20th century with Dixieland,
progressed to big band swing, then Bebop, post-Bebop, Free Jazz, Fusion, and so forth.

Prophecies of War is a multimedia production. Musically, it is a multi-movement Progressive/Jazz-Fusion/Jazz
Rock. Harmonically it covers many of the ecclesiastical modes. Since it's first performance, Prophecies of War
and its subsequent movements were edited and expanded. Initially Prophecies of War performance time was just over
30 minutes. During it's final revision and performance, the performance time lasted almost 2 hours.

In the Beginning is an upbeat odd metered composition centered around E Lydian and is the first movement
of the entire production. The improvisation section is an open form requiring the bass guitarist to lay down a
Jazz-Fusion styled bass line. In live performances, after the solos were complete, I would return and play a simple
melody hinting at the melody of the second movement. During this musical transition, the band would modulate to
B Aeolian.

And with all that said . . . enjoy.

Andrew Hanna

Score

In the Beginning

Andrew Hanna

14
Alto Sax.
Dr.
E. Gtr.
E. Bass
Kbd.
Ped.
18
B
In time ♪. =120
Alto Sax.
Dr.
E. Gtr.
E. Bass
B
In time ♪. =120
Kbd.
Ped.
Ped.
Ped.

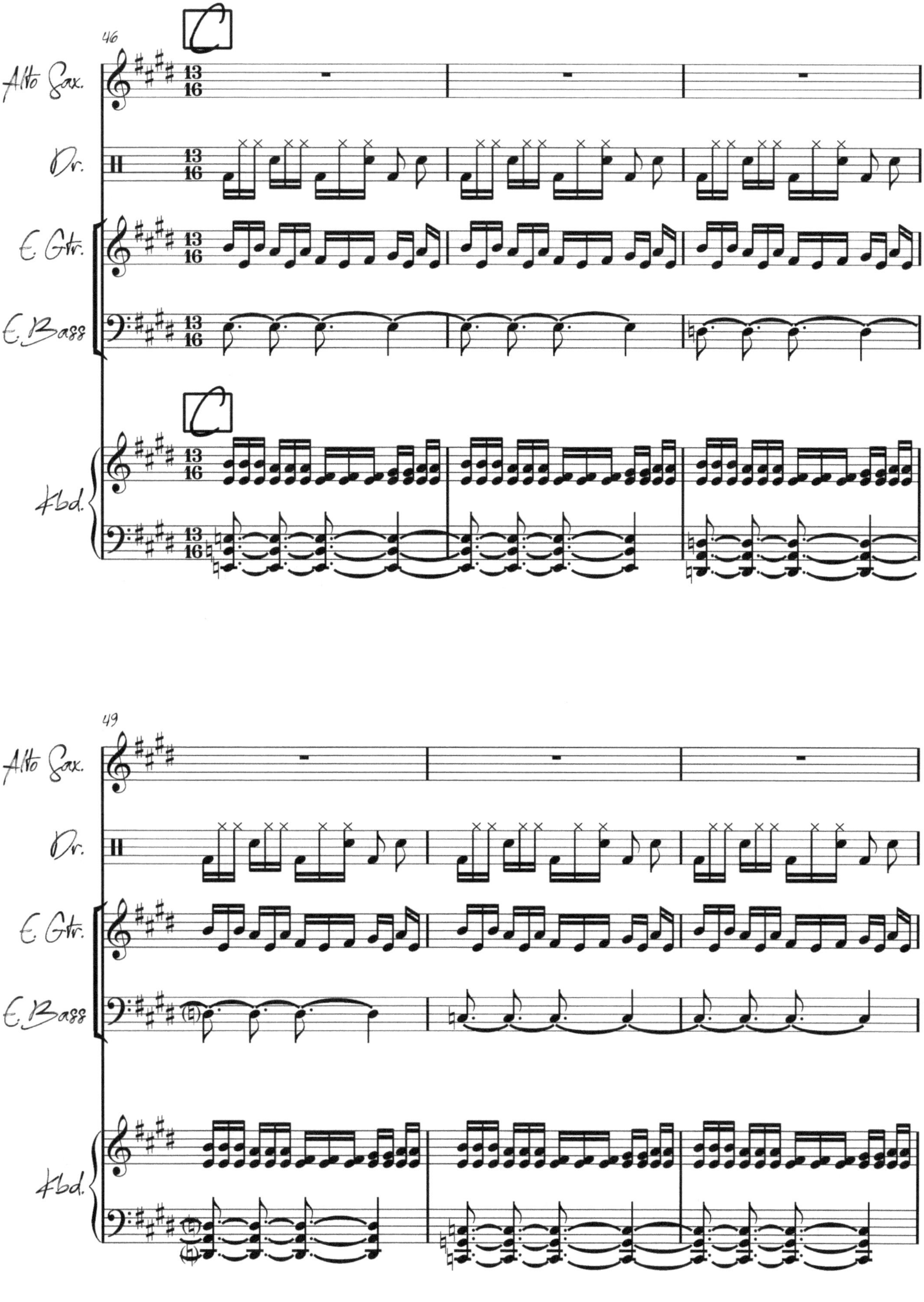
46
C
Alto Sax.
Dr.
E. Gtr.
E. Bass
Kbd.
13
16
49

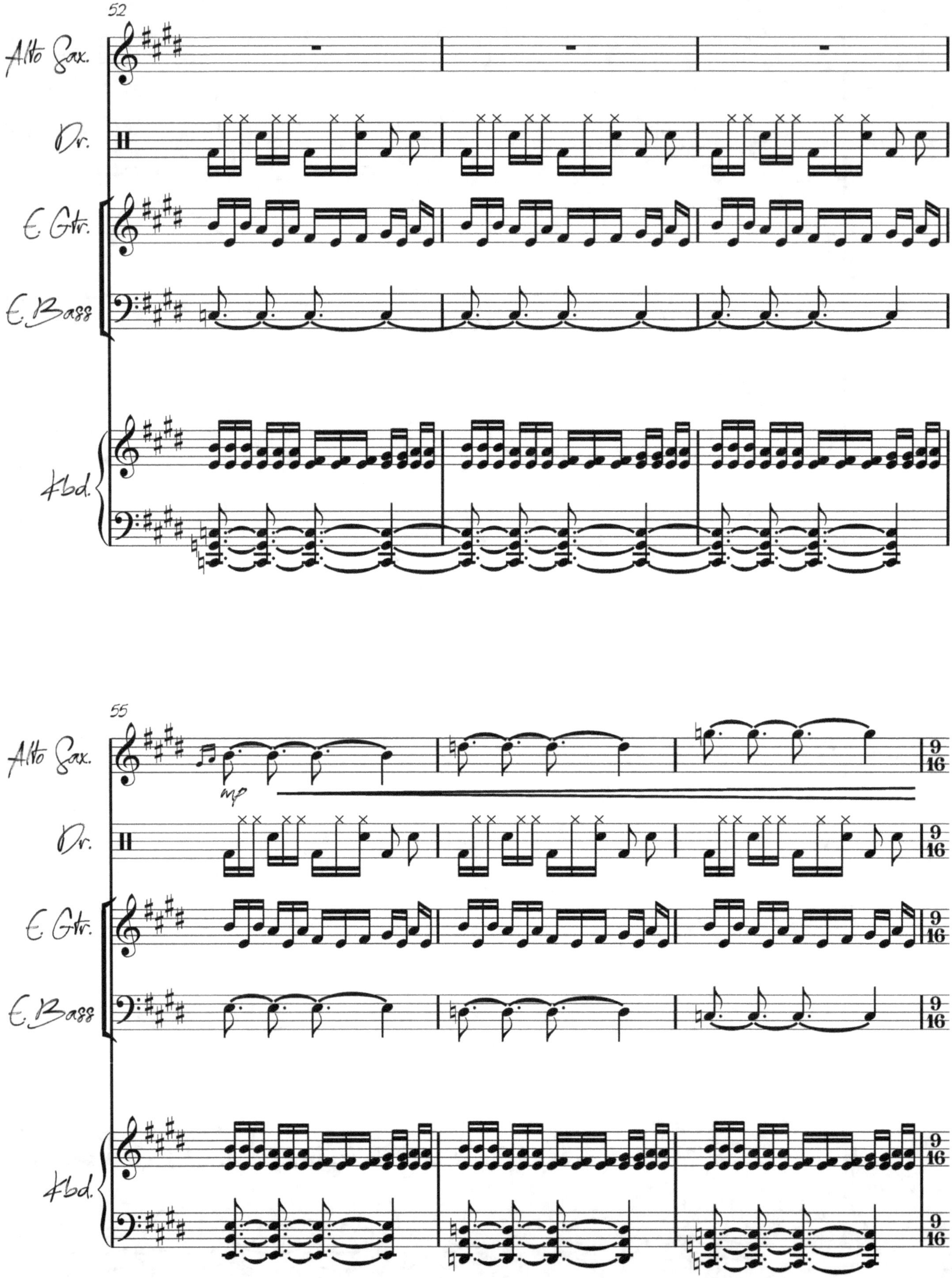
52
Alto Sax.
Dr.
E. Gtr.
E. Bass
Kbd.
55
Alto Sax.
mp
Dr.
E. Gtr.
E. Bass
Kbd.
9
16

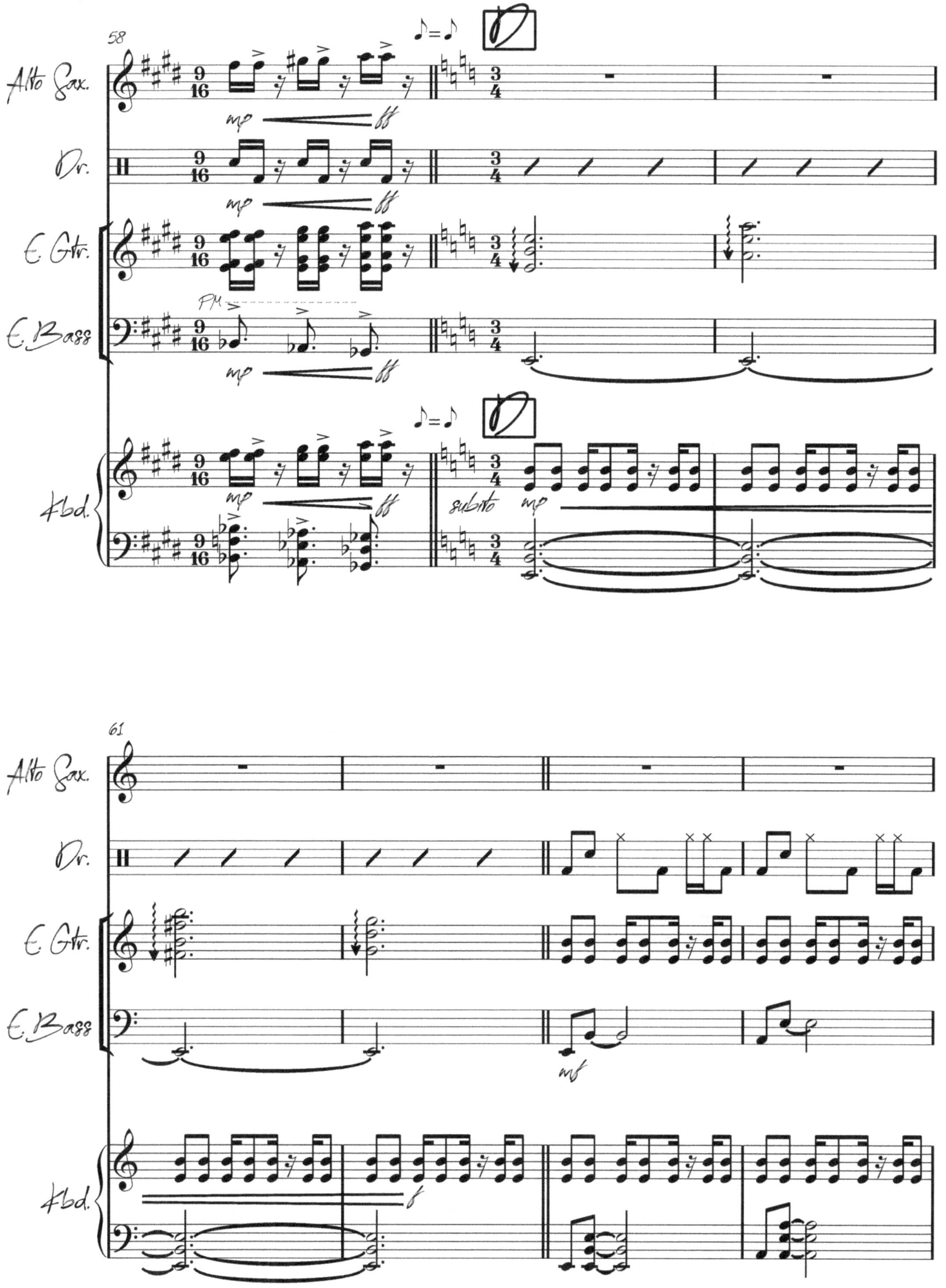
58
D
Alto Sax.
Dr.
E. Gtr.
E. Bass
Kbd.
mp
ff
PM
subito
mp
61
f
mf

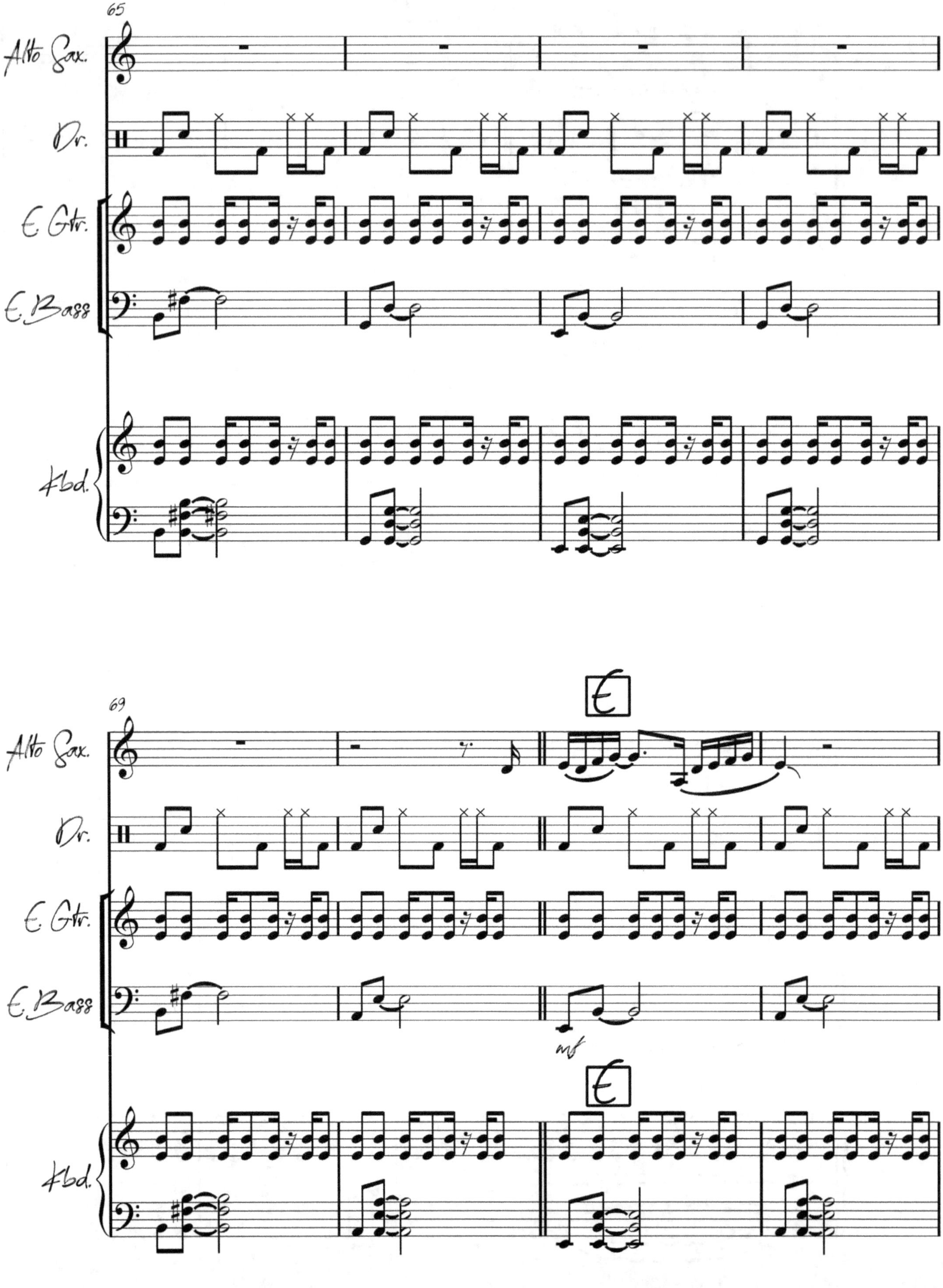
65
Alto Sax.
Dr.
E. Gtr.
E. Bass
Kbd.
69
E
mf

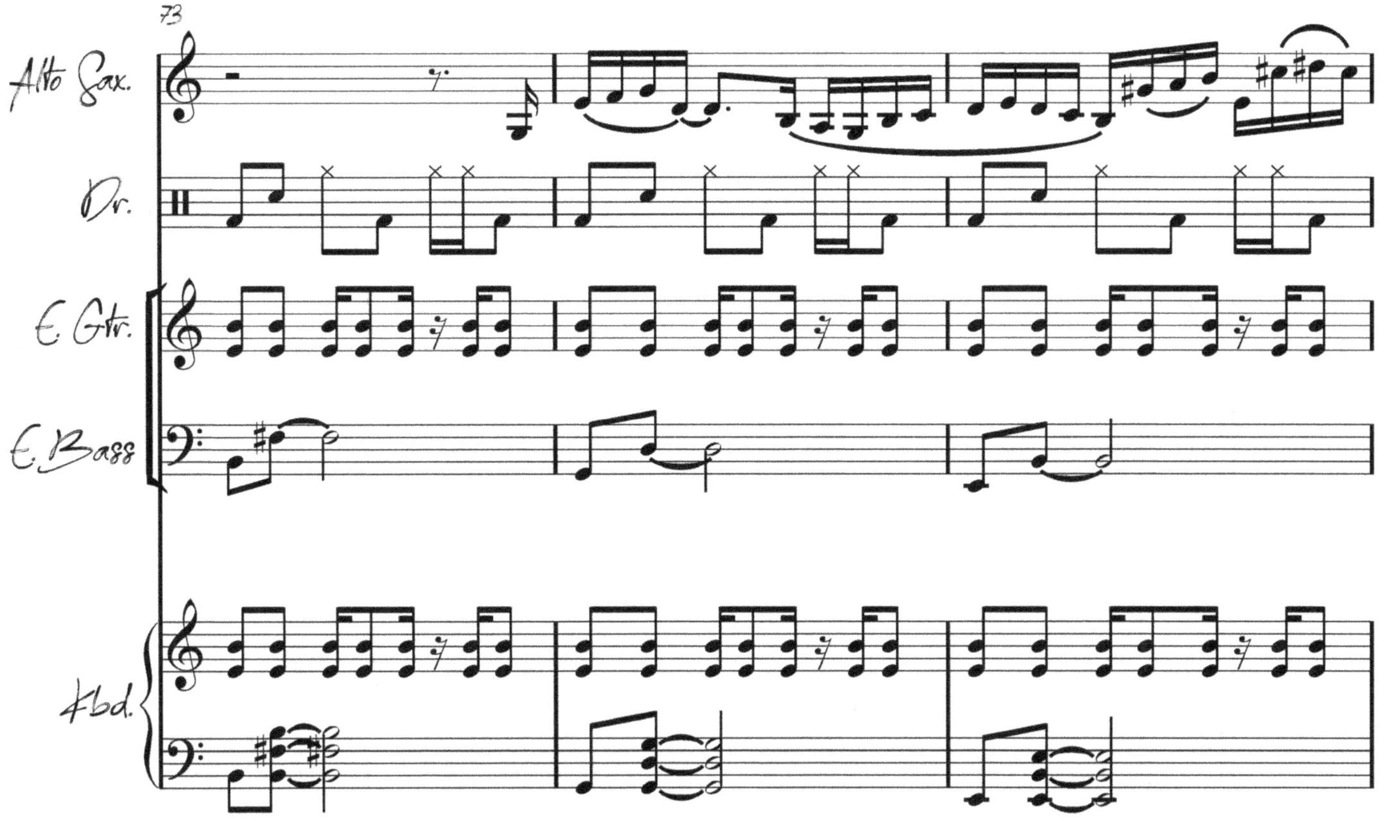
73
Alto Sax.
Dr.
E. Gtr.
E. Bass
Kbd.

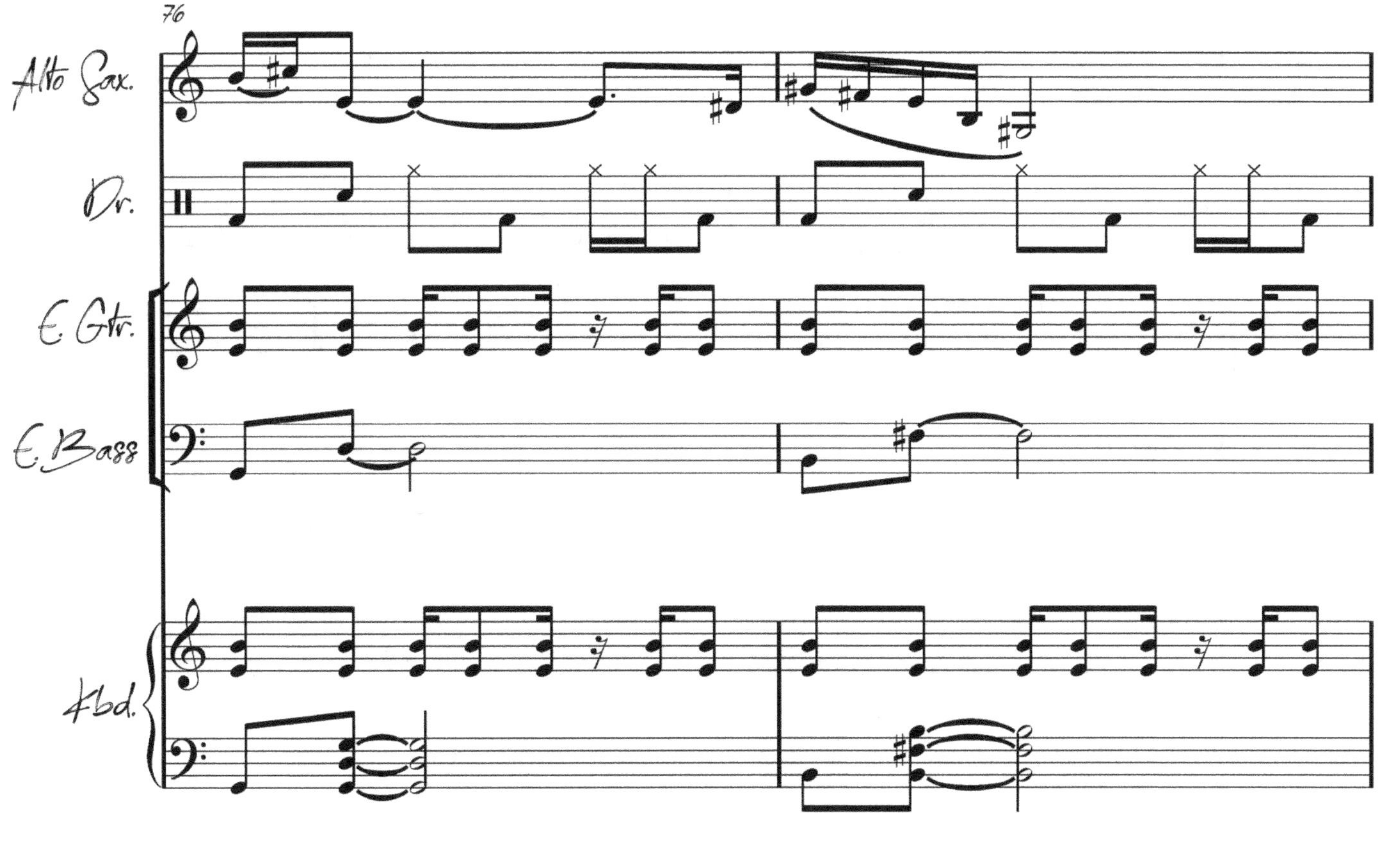
76
Alto Sax.
Dr.
E. Gtr.
E. Bass
Kbd.

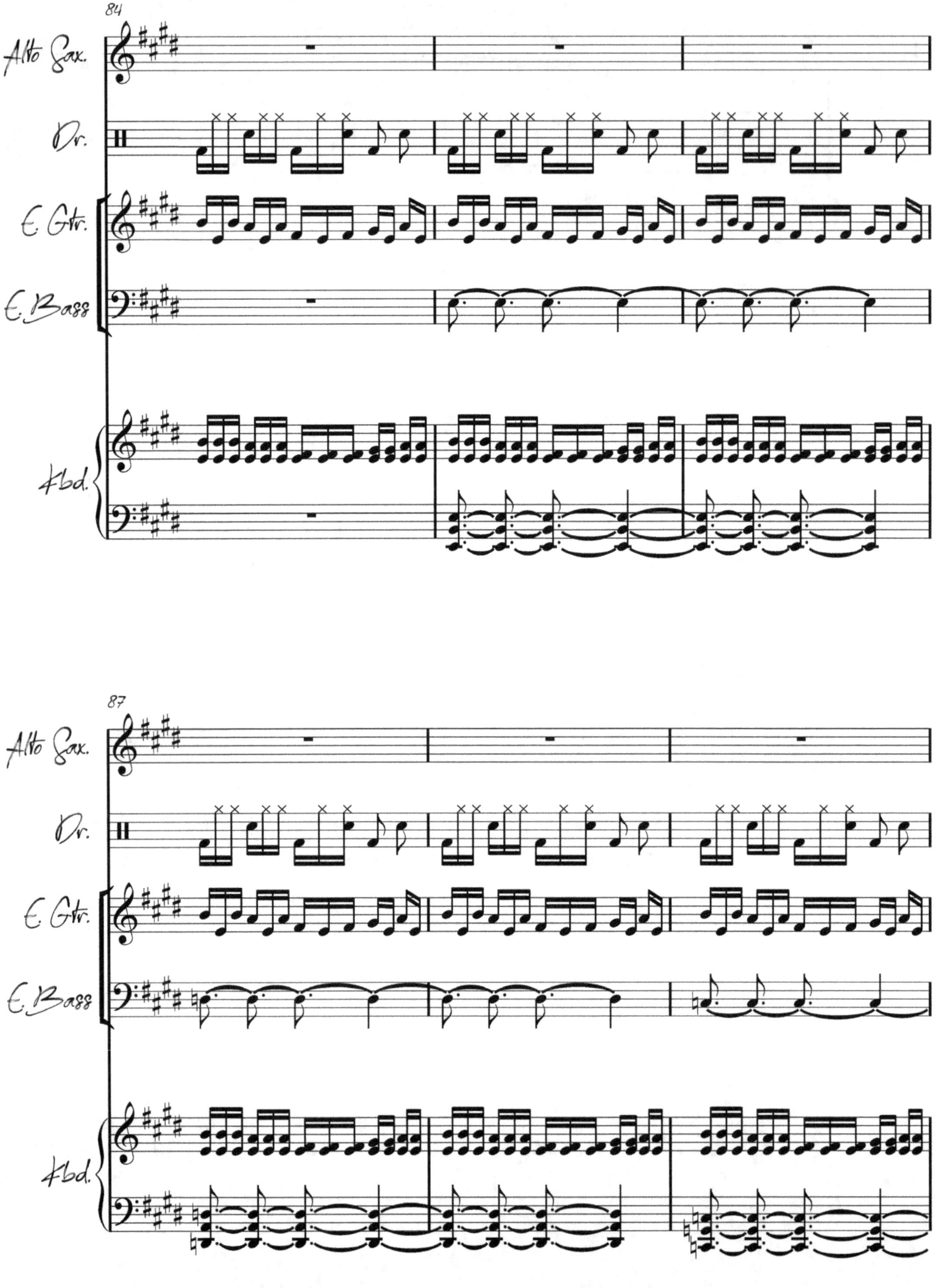
84
Alto Sax.
Dr.
E. Gtr.
E. Bass
Kbd.
87
Alto Sax.
Dr.
E. Gtr.
E. Bass
Kbd.

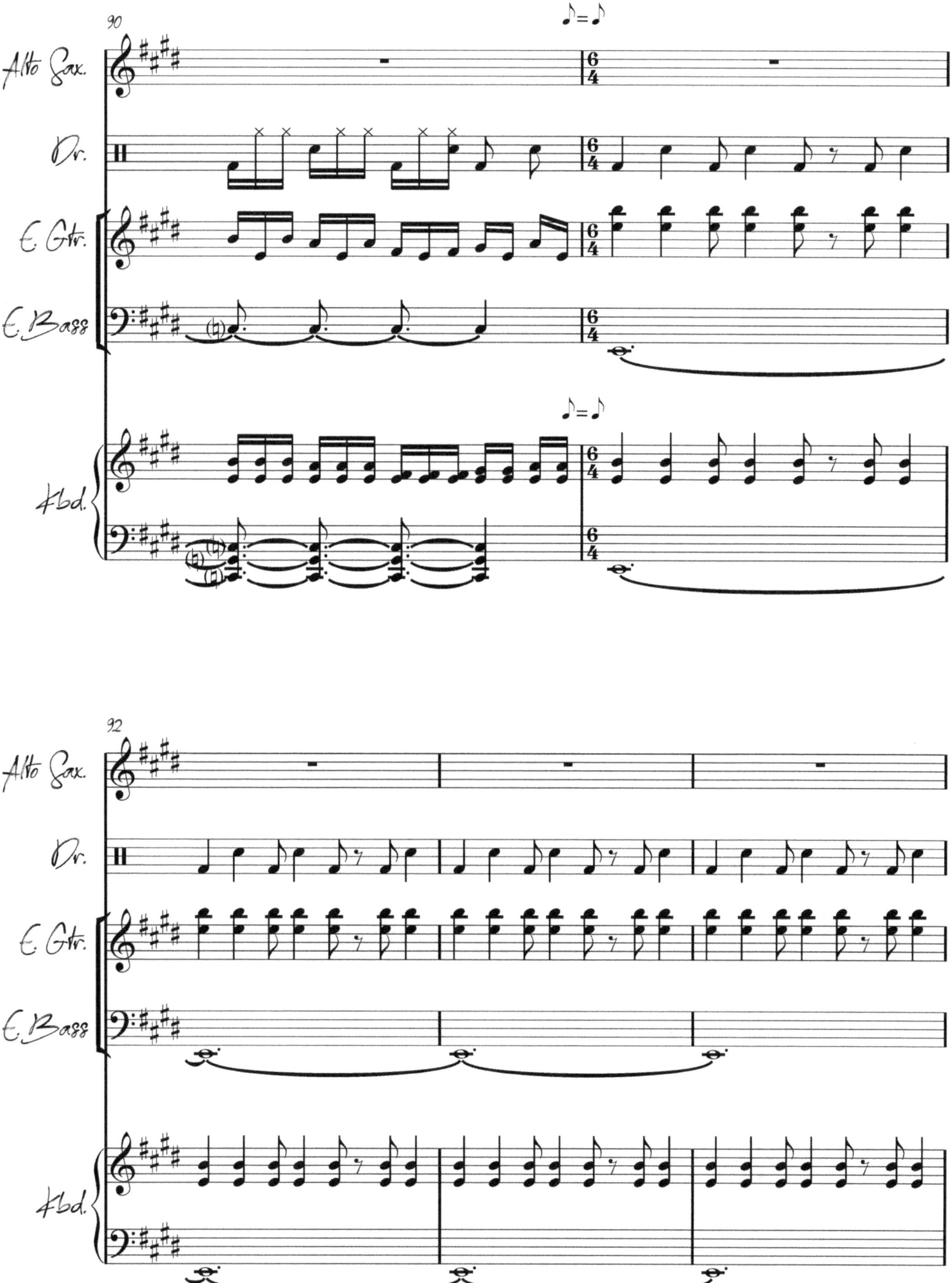

90
♪=♪
Alto Sax.
Dr.
E. Gtr.
E. Bass
♪=♪
Kbd.
92
Alto Sax.
Dr.
E. Gtr.
E. Bass
Kbd.

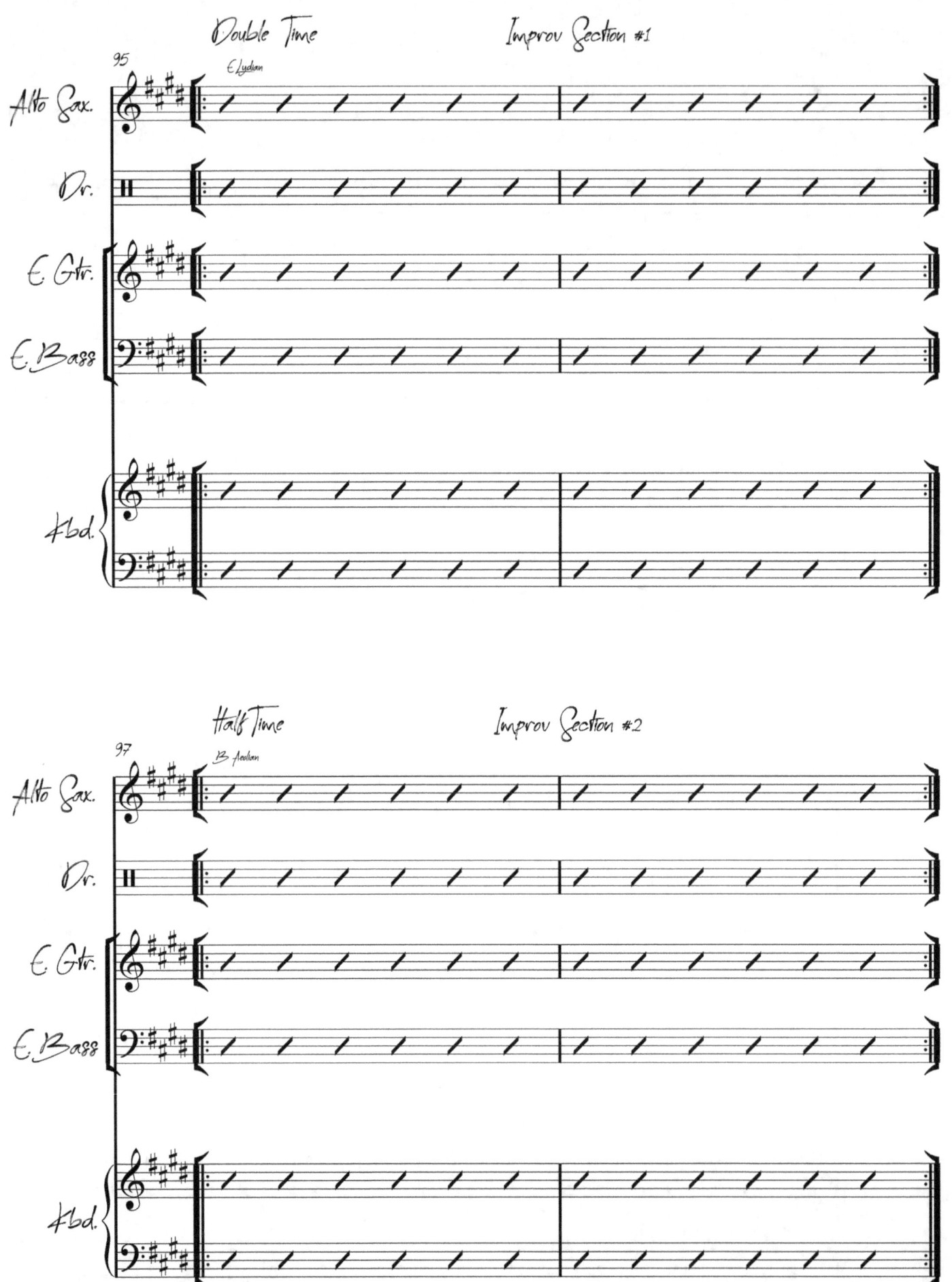

Alto Saxophone

In the Beginning

Alto Saxophone

Andrew Hanna

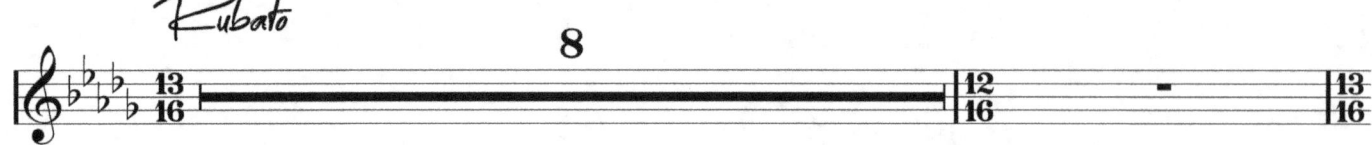

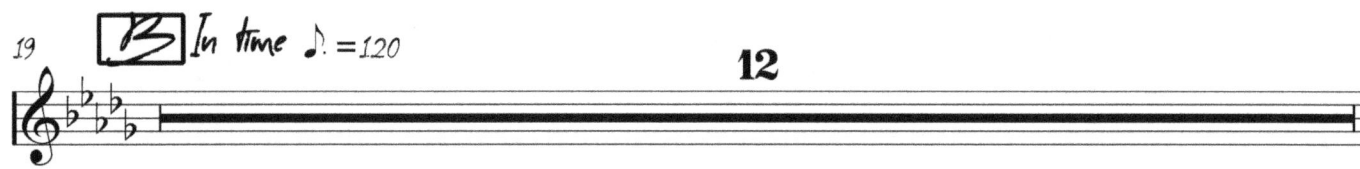

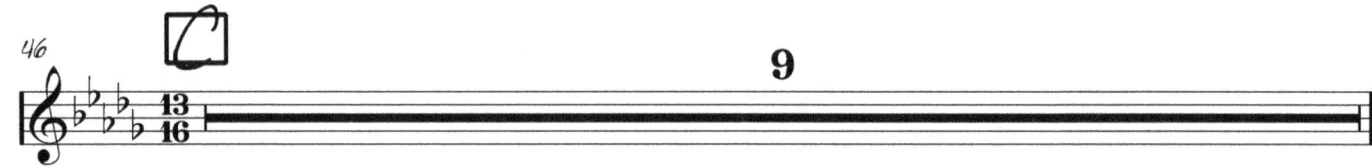

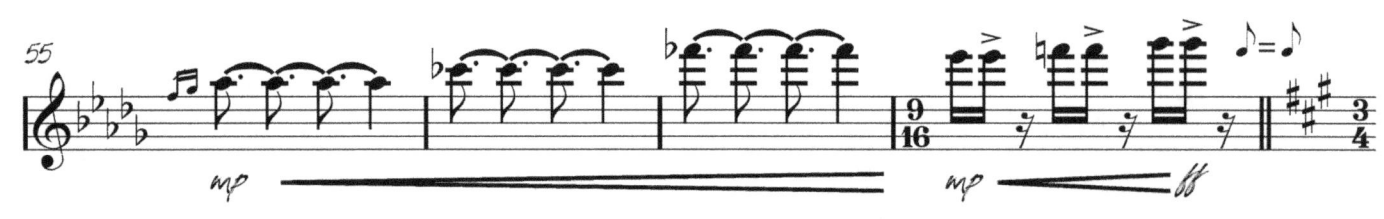

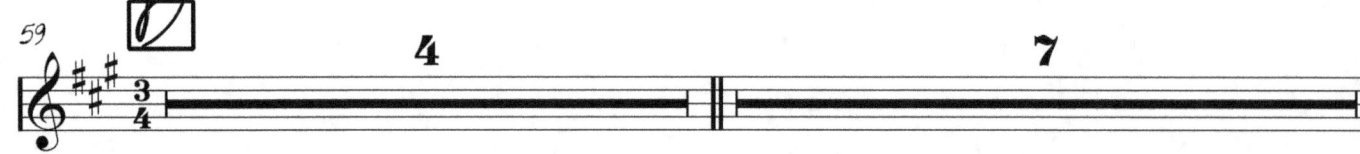

Alto Saxophone

Drum Set

In the Beginning

Drum Set

Andrew Hanna

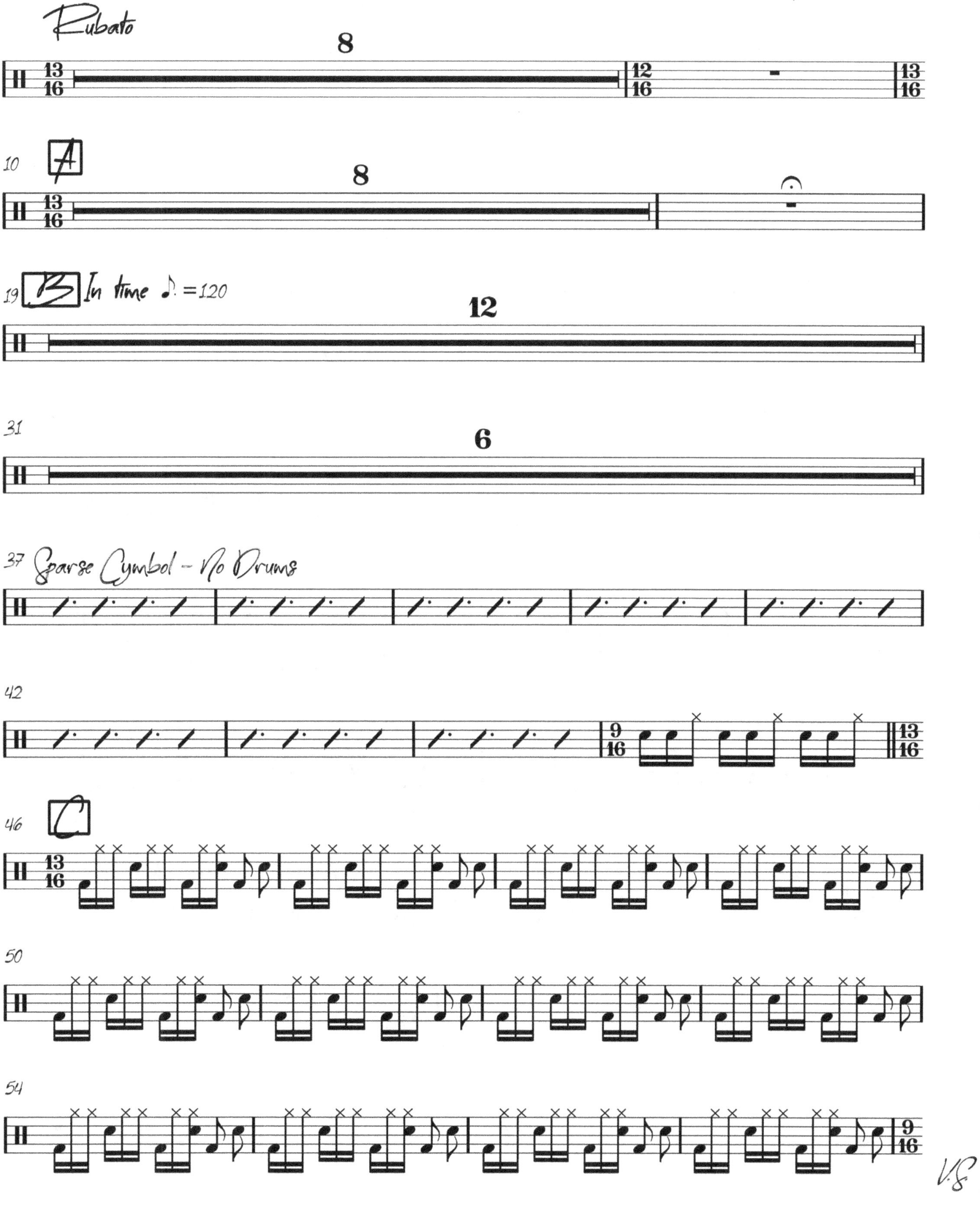

Electric Bass

Electric Bass

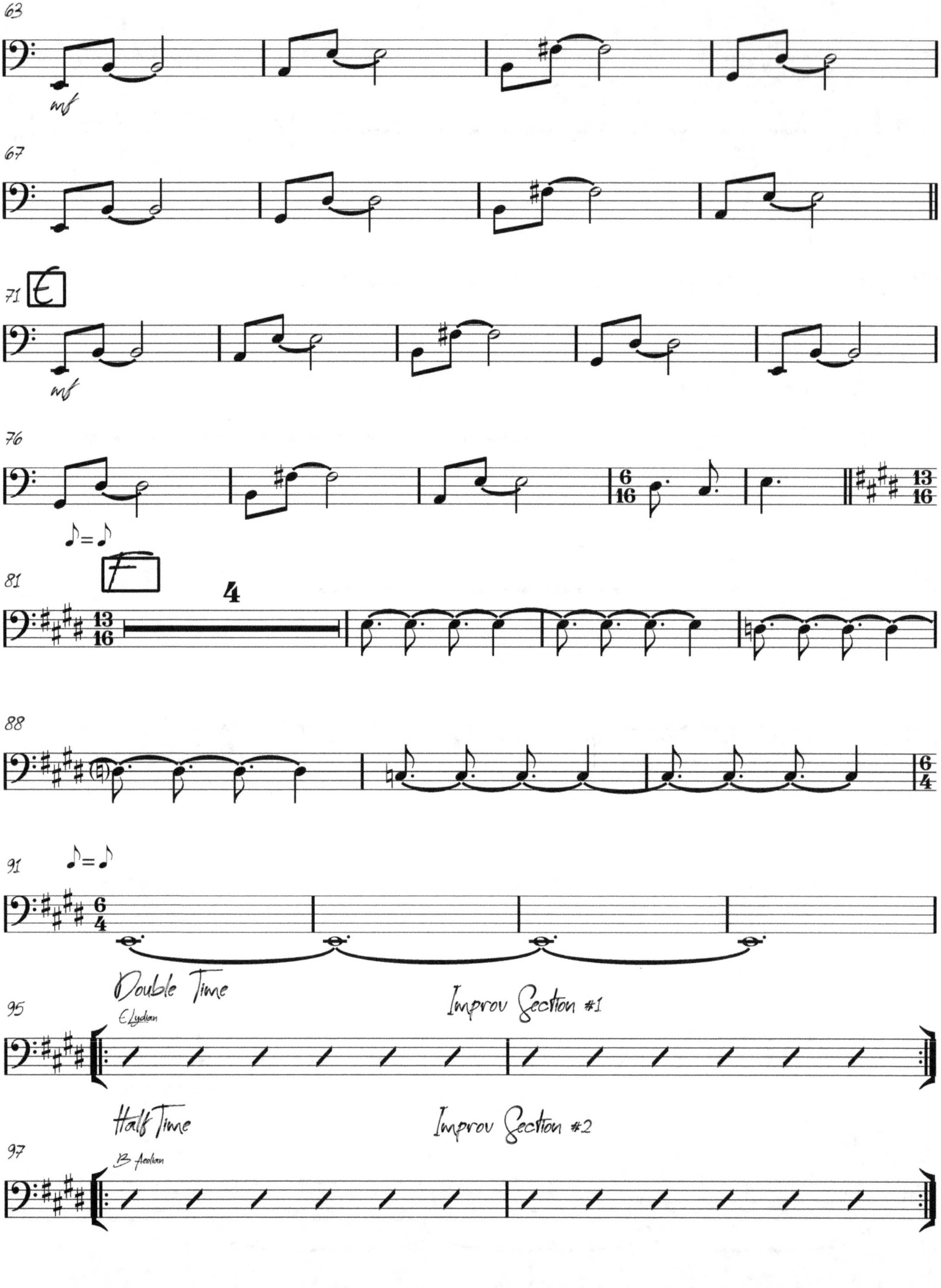

Electric Guitar

In the Beginning

Electric Guitar

Andrew Hanna

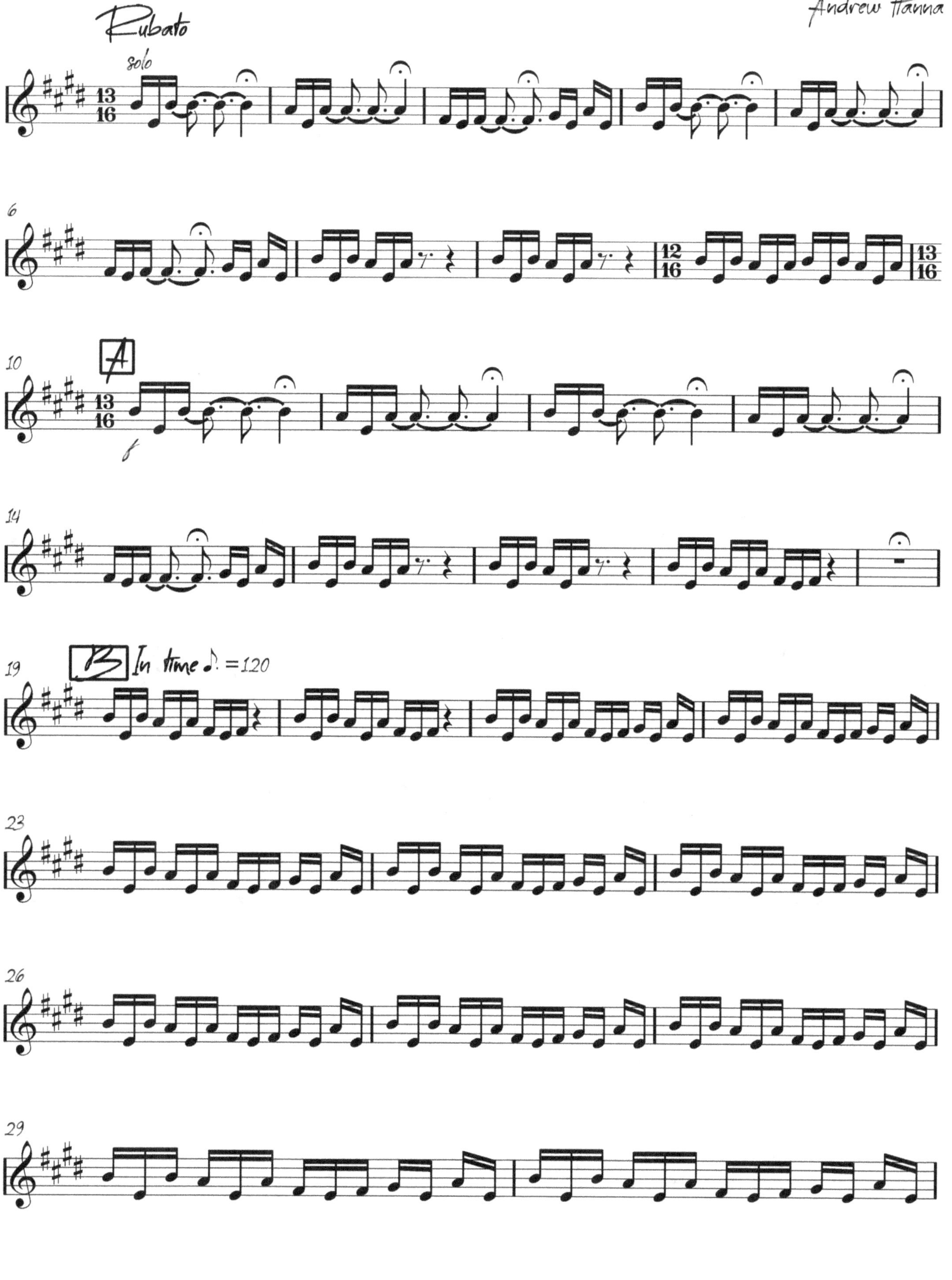

Electric Guitar

Electric Guitar

Keyboards

In the Beginning

Keyboard

Andrew Hanna

V.S.

Keyboard

Keyboard

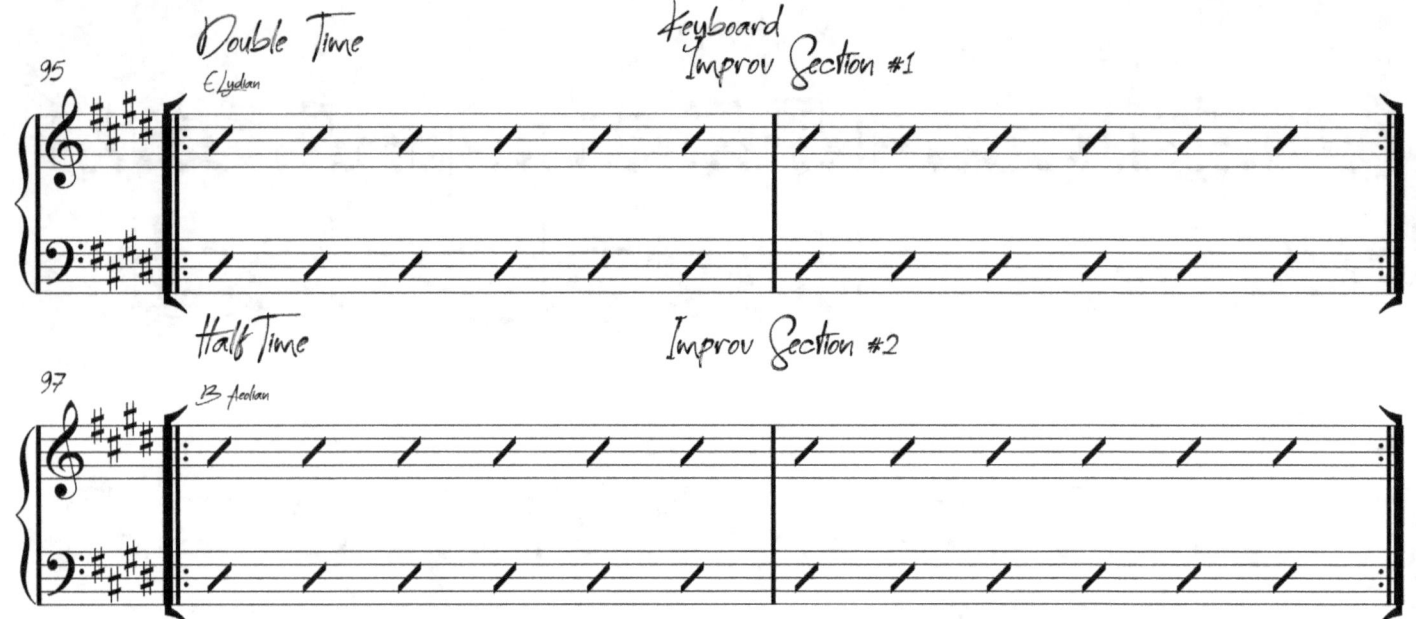

www.ingramcontent.com/pod-product-compliance
Lightning Source LLC
Chambersburg PA
CBHW081010120626
46546CB00010B/3099